# AT THE PAPER GATES
# WITH BURNING DESIRE

## Other Poetry Books by Carlota Caulfield

*Fanaim* (1984)

*Oscuridad divina* (1985, 1987)

*A veces me llamo infancia /*
*Sometimes I Call Myself Childhood* (1985)

*El tiempo es una mujer que espera* (1986)

*34th Street and other poems* (1987)

*Angel Dust / Polvo de Angel / Polvere d'Angelo* (1990)

*Estrofas de papel, barro y tinta* (1995)

*A las puertas del papel con amoroso fuego* (1996)

*Libro de los XXXIX escalones / Book of the XXXIX Steps* (1997)

*Book of the XXXIX Steps: A Poetry Game*
*of Discovery and Imagination.* CD-ROM (1999)

*Quincunce* (2001)

*Autorretrato en ojo ajeno* (2001)

Carlota Caulfield

# AT THE PAPER GATES
# WITH BURNING DESIRE

Translated by Angela McEwan
in collaboration with the Author

Eboli Poetry
*An Imprint of* InteliBooks *Publishers*

Cover Design: Damion Gordon - BTP Graphx
Cover illustration: "Les épîtres d'Ovide." French, early sixteenth century.
Bibliothèque Nationale, Paris.
Cover photo of the Author with Anne Bonnie by S.G.

English translation of *A las puertas del papel con amoroso fuego*, published by
Ediciones Torremozas, Madrid, 1996.

ISBN 0-9711391-2-1 (softcover)

This book was printed in the United States of America
To order additional copies of this book, contact:

**InteliBooks**
www.InteliBooks.com
Orders@InteliBooks.com

*For Afán*

*A las puertas del papel con amoroso fuego* received a Poetry Mention at the "Premio Plural" of Mexico City in 1992. The book received the Honorable Mention in the 1997 Latino Literature Prize for published books in Poetry awarded by the Latin American Writers Institute of New York.

Acknowledgments are made to the editors of the following publications in which some of these poems appeared: *Beacons*; *The Texas Review*; *Brújula/Compass*; *Walrus*.

# Contents

# Opening the Gates of Carlota Caulfield's Poetry

Women have written and still write love letters on the hidden, tattooed backs of their loved ones, on pillows embroidered with the following words: "I think only of you, beloved," and so many times, when it was impossible for them to sail, or rather because they were not allowed to travel, they wrote letters to put in blue bottles. Since the 16th century the epistolary genre has been recognized as a powerful form of literary expression. Women have always written love letters to real or imaginary recipients, secret perfumed letters written in blood and ink, pens with which to live and be in the world. Love letters were also the inner message of passionate, secretive women.

Carlota Caulfield, both ancient and modern in her enigmatic presence, as well as in her writing, has traveled through visible and invisible cities to establish a dialogue with the fluid, suggestive body of letters by women, known and unknown, in love and rejected. She searched for the voice and words of Lucrezia Borgia, Maria Savorgnan, a virgin of the sun, an unpublished letter of Nora's, and the body's textures. Through them, she has recreated her own text: a beguiling, suggestive dialogue of love.

These letters of our sisters and the poet Carlota Caulfield, are a true alliance of sisterhood as well as a celebration of the feminine imagination through its most sacred tradition: love letters. These letters are rooted in the body of desire itself, and rendered in the body of the text by means of the voice, which having heard and read, recreates them with subtle wisdom and passion in the ecstatic *corpus* of her own writing.

The sequence of poems reveals a beautiful and thought-provoking dialogue of the written word through the ages and through memory, uniting in the passionate, intense voice of the writer. To read these love letters of other women is to create them anew in the voice of one's own being. For example, Sor Mariana writes to her beloved because, "I feel I'm talking to you as I write and receiving the benefit of your presence," that presence which will be transformed through the poet's voice in the extension of the other woman's letter, which later will become one and the same story. Caulfield in the same letter states the following: "I believed in your hands / which are sweet (...) /I write to cure myself / of my madness," and perhaps this is the essential redeeming phrase of the texts.

Writing as a way of fighting absence or invoking a presence: writing in order to avoid gesticulating passionately and to simply be. In another letter, Flora Tristán, the tireless traveler, states: "...the young man I loved completely (...) was one of those cold and calculating beings, for whom a great passion always bore the appearance of madness: he was afraid of my love." Caulfield recreates Flora Tristán and herself gravitating to the edge of zones of devastating passion, the zones of madness and delirium, unrequited passion fatally marked with indifference: "Sometimes we women /with a disguise of indifference/ make ourselves queens,/ but you well know that / a declaration of love / can be fatal."

These texts are beautiful, suggestive, terrifying and humorous. For example, the one devoted to the Countess Pardo Bazán in which Caulfield recreates the history of the inside gossip and suggestive secrets contained in love letters, as if they were magnets of memory. Rosa Luxemburg, Flora Tristán, Gabriela Mistral, Isadora Duncan and many other women appear as diligent, roving travelers in deep discussion with the poet who is the reader, and at the same time is the body of other women, like the letters of her own love and her daguerreotypes: "I have Mozart and Schubert / at my fingertips."

Carlota Caulfield has recreated and created a moving collection of poems in which the scene or the landscape of the scene or the landscape of the written word, is in itself a great poem, a beautiful act of love and faith. The letters in this collection are passages from stories within stories and are, more than anything, a moving way of coming closer to the mysterious enchantment of the letters, which are like figures looking at themselves and being transformed "The noon music left me powerless: / *the falling water wears away rock* / and I thought perhaps we could change roles / Venetian Masks, wind blowing within me, / any glance at your naked body..."

Carlota Caulfield gives us an extraordinary and hallucinatory book, original and disturbing, which helps us to recreate our madness and love as extraordinary women of a universal history, from countesses to dancers, from Incan princesses to nuns, because this poet knows that the true secret of love letters does not lie with the recipient, but with the writer. This is an exquisite and joyous collection, a classic work of 20th century poetry. Caulfield is a poet to read and remember: her love letters will forever be in the secret zones or in the open landscapes of the written word.

Marjorie Agosin

*and broken*
*the tongue is silent, while the hand writes*
—Sappho

## Poemas tatuados

I
Zaida se confunde por los caminos de Dios
con mi manto de pelusa cenicienta
que revolotea sobre nuestro *liso cuerpo de cobre*
mientras por debajo del velo
me hablas de amor.

II
La escritura de mi cuerpo
es una rica capa con hombreras.
a la moda de Bagdad.
La derecha escribe mi independencia,
mientras la izquierda es tu lectura
de mis versos y como recompensa, un beso.

*(Wallada, 994-1091)*

.

## Tattooed Poems

I
Zaida disappears down God's roads
with my gray plush cape
fluttering over our *smooth copper body*
while beneath the veil
you speak to me of love.

II
The writing of my body
is a rich broad-shouldered cape,
Baghdad style.
The right shoulder proclaims my independence,
while the left is your reading
of my verses, rewarded by a kiss.

*(Wallada, 994-1091)*

## Carta de Lucrezia Borgia
## a su confesor

padre, si usted fuera mujer
entendería las razones
y no me haría decir tantas avemarías.
padre, ¿no se da cuenta?
mi castigo de ahora
es libertad en el siglo XX.

## Letter From Lucrezia Borgia
## to Her Confessor

Father, if you were a woman
you would understand the reasons
and not make me say so many Ave Marías.
Father, don't you see?
My punishment now
is twentieth century freedom.

## Un día de conversaciones
## con algunos personajes venecianos

Nanna le dice a Pippa
que
nuestra prudencia es
un teatro de cartón
lleno de memorias
que nos regala Giulio Camillo.

En tus transformaciones
hoy me pareces un *ready-made*
y ayer una hoja en blanco
a punto de ser escrita por muchas plumas.

*(Pietro Aretino me ha dicho, y hablo de 1548,*
*que te vio cerca de la iglesia de San Juan)*

## A Day of Conversations
## with some Venetian Personalities

Nanna tells Pippa
that
prudence for us is
a cardboard theater
filled with memories
given us by Giulio Camillo.

In your transformations
today you seem a ready-made
and yesterday a blank sheet
about to be written on by many pens.

*(Pietro Aretino has told me, and I'm speaking in
1548, that he saw you near the church of St.
John)*

## Carta de Camilla de Pisa
## a Francesco del Nero

¡QUE DIOS castigue con toda clase de castigos a esa mujer que en este mismo instante posee aquello que me es más querido en este siglo XVI! Maldigo las noches y todos los instantes que pasas en otros brazos que no son los míos. Malditos sean los besos y todos los actos que me causan tanto dolor. Dios mío, dame paciencia. No hay nada que yo pueda hacer.

*(Traducción libre sin dedicatoria)*

## Letter from Camilla of Pisa
## to Francesco del Nero

MAY GOD inflict all kinds of punishment on the woman who at this very moment possesses that which I most love in this sixteenth century! I curse the nights and every instant you spend in other arms than mine. Cursed be the kisses and all the acts that cause me so much pain. My God, give me patience. There is nothing I can do.

*(Free translation without dedication)*

# Mi última carta es

para dejar mi vestido amarillo
mi escudo de armas
mis cincuenta y una perlas
mis poemas y mis cartas
a aquel que una tarde de enero,
en Piazza San Marco,
se miró en mis ojos
sin decirme nada...

*Verónica del Cinquecento*

## My Last Letter is

to leave my yellow dress
my coat of arms
my fifty-one pearls
my poems and my letters
to the man who one January afternoon,
in the Piazza San Marco,
looked deep into my eyes
without saying a word...


Veronica del Cinquecento

## Carta de María Savorgnan a Pietro Bembo
### escrita alrededor de 1500

Quiero una palabrita de tu mano. Me has dicho que ardes y yo te digo que *ardo e non so che arder più si posi.*

## Letter from Maria Savorgnan to Pietro Bembo
*written about 1500*

I want a little word written by you. You have told me you burn and I tell you that *ardo e non so che arder piú si posi.*

## Il fine della terza e ultima giornata

Te escribo desde Venecia, Edina querida, y aquí me quedo. Me he fatigado de andar en trenes. R llega mañana y quizás se queda hasta el Carnaval. Envíame toda la correspondencia que me llegue a Ackermannstrasse al Hotel Granturco. Muchos besos para ti y un abrazo muy fuerte para el Terrible.

*(Tarjeta postal enviada por la actriz irlandesa Lotti Cathmhaoil a su amiga la pintora suiza Hedwig Von Aregger poco antes de que LC se convirtiera en Urganda la Desconocida)*

## Il fine della terza e ultima giornata

I write to you from Venice, dear Edina, and here
I remain. I am exhausted from traveling on
trains. R arrives tomorrow and perhaps will stay
until Carnival. Forward to the Granturco Hotel
all the mail that arrives for me at Ackermannstrasse. Lots of kisses for you and a big hug for
the Terrible One.

*(Post card sent by the Irish actress Lotti Cathmhaoil
to her friend, Hedwig Von Aregger, the Swiss
painter, shortly before L.C. turned into Urganda
the Unknown)*

## *Todo beso a mujer honesta es un atentado*

Marco *di Piero di Batista da Ortignano per
havere per forza baciato una fanciulla da marito
nella strada.*
(Exiliado en Pisa por cinco años bajo la pena
de dos años de galeras, parag. III, art. 81, Edit.
general-Gob.Roma, 1540)


Por haberme besado, querido amigo,
tienes varios años de buena suerte
y pasas a la posteridad inmaculado.
Debo decirte que admiro varias cosas de ti:
tu manera de vestirte,
tus brazos, la curva de tus labios,
tu sonrisa de niño salvaje,
tu buen apetito y el no haber
contestado mis cartas.

## Kissing a Honest Woman
## is an Affront

*Marco di Piero di Batista da Ortignano per havere per forza baciato una fanciulla da marito nella strada.*
(Exiled to Pisa for five years under sentence of two years in the galleys. *Paragraph III, art. 81. Edit. general-Gob. Roma, 1540*)


For having kissed me, dear friend,
you have several years of good luck
and will be immaculate forever.
I should tell you I admire several things about
you:
your way of dressing,
your arms, the curve of your lips,
your wild child's smile,
your good appetite and your not having
answered my letters.

## Cantiga 140

Mientras yo, Madonna Elisabetta Rusconi,
en mi diminuto taller
de la *Calle dei Cinque*
imprimía libros hebreos,
tú ibas encima de una góndola
loando a Santa María.

## Song 140

While I, Madonna Elisabetta Rusconi,
in my tiny workshop
on *Calle dei Cinque*
printed books in Hebrew,
you floated on a gondola
singing the praises of St. Mary.

## Carta de una virgen del sol
## a su amante

En una tinaja
escondo el quipú
con la historia
y los sonidos
de nuestros besos.
Querido mío,
guarda bien la cinta de mi talle.
Piensa en mi pelo y en sus adornos.
Yo pienso en ti y te aseguro
que muy prontico sobornaré a mamaogro
para seguir tejiendo de colores tu cuerpo
a mi cuerpo.


*(Para Abraham)*

## Letter from a Virgin of the Sun
## to her Lover

In a clay jug
I hide the quipu strings
with the history
and the sounds
of our kisses.
My dearest,
take good care of the ribbon from my waist.
Think of my hair and its ornaments.
I think of you and I assure you
that very, very soon I'll bribe mama ogre,
the priestess
so I can go on weaving our bodies together
with colors.

*(For Abraham)*

## Encerrada en Pastrana en 1585, pienso en ti

Antonio de mis amores
alcanzo el punto central de la Rueda.
Recorro la síntesis de una noche
contigo desnudo en mis brazos:
¡Qué muera el Rey!
Hablemos de política,
destruyamos las convenciones
y amémonos, que el tiempo es poco.

Vuela la paloma
sobre mi recinto de sombras.
Mi ojo izquierdo sigue siendo
el décimo arcano del Tarot.
El último abrazo
de mi vida mortal
tiene una túnica naranja.

¿Quién dijo aquello de
Post coitum, animal triste?

A mí me llaman Eboli, la profeta.

## Locked up in Pastrana in 1585,
## I Think of You

My beloved Antonio
I reach the center point of the Wheel.
I retrace the synthesis of a night
with you naked in my arms:
Down with the King!
Let us talk of politics,
let us destroy conventions
and let us love each other, for time is short.

The dove flies
over my shadowy alcove.
My left eye is still
the tenth mystery of Tarot.
The last embrace
of my mortal life
has an orange tunic.

Who was it said
*Post coitum*, sad flesh?

They call me Eboli, the prophetess.

## Intertexto de nuestro idilio

¿Qué más da que me llame
Lotti, Aennchen, Isabel o Margarita?

¿Qué importancia tiene
el habernos conocido
en Weimar, Zürich, Marienband,
Berna o Venecia?

¿Qué más da que te llames Werther,
Frederick, Rodolfo o Fausto?

¿Qué importa todo si ya no te amo?


*(Fax marcado urgente)*

## Intertext of Our Idyll

What matter if I call myself
Lotti, Aennchen, Isabella or Margaret?

What's the difference
if we met
in Weimar, Zürich, Marienbad,
Bern or Venice?

What matter if your name is Werther,
Frederick, Rudolf or Faust?

What does anything matter if I no longer love you?


*(Fax marked urgent)*

*(Encontrado entre los papeles inéditos de George Sand. Se cree que esta carta fue escrita en Mallorca en medio de su pasión por Federico)*

Respiro y descanso
al mirarte desnudo.
Este acompañarnos y saber callar
por los caminos de nuestro dolor:
mi escritura se teje
sobre las paredes
del incomparable acorde de tus manos.

*(Found Among the Private Papers of George Sand. It is Believed that this Letter was Written on Mallorca at the Height of Her Passion for Federico)*

I inhale and relax
when I see you naked.
Keeping each other company in silence
through the paths of our pain:
my writing is woven
on the walls
of the matchless harmony of your hands.

# *Los Maestros Cantores: telegrama*

De crepúsculo a crepúsculo
gozo cada vez que te escribo
y me doy cuenta de que
no hay un ideal masculino.

## The Meistersingers: Telegram

From dusk to dusk
it pleases me when I write to you
and realize
there is no masculine ideal.

## Ne credere Byron

Siempre me he sentido como Carolina Lamb
desde que vi aquella película en La Habana.
Yo también me he disfrazado de cochero,
he hablado en idiomas extraños,
he falsificado identificaciones y
he escrito cartas apasionadas,
para despertar sobre tu pecho.

## Ne credere Byron

Ever since I saw that film in Havana
I've felt like Caroline Lamb.
I too have disguised myself as a coach driver,
spoken in strange tongues,
forged identity papers and
written passionate letters
to wake up on your chest.

## *Yo me escribo: Cartas de amor de Sor Mariana al conde Noël de Chamilly, Chez Barbin, 1669*

Primera Carta

*¿Te alegrabas de tener una pasión tan intensa como la mía?*

Huí de oraciones
y detuve la historia
del convento
para decirte te quiero.
Tu última carta
volvió a mentir,
y mi corazón,
difícil de entender,
voló a tu encuentro.

## I Write to Myself: Love Letters from Sor Mariana to Count Noël de Chamilly, Chez Barbin, 1669

First Letter

*Were you overjoyed to have a passion as intense as mine?*

I fled from prayers
and interrupted the history
of the convent
to tell you I love you.
Your last letter
lied again,
and my heart,
so hard to understand,
flew to meet you.

## Segunda Carta

*Parece que te hablo mientras te escribo y que logro el bien de tu presencia*

Creí en tus manos
que son dulces
que corren como avecillas
que santificaron mi cuerpo.
Te escribo para escapar de ti.
Te escribo para destruir
el espejismo de tu sombra.
Escribo para curarme
de mi locura.

Second Letter

*I feel I'm talking to you as I write and receiving
the benefit of your presence*

I believed in your hands
which are sweet
which run down my body
like little birds, sanctifying it.
I write to you to escape from you.
I write to you to destroy
the mirage of your shadow.
I write to cure myself
of my madness.

## Tercera Carta

*No sé por qué te escribo*

Si no te lo mereces
por débil de alma.
Tus prometidas cartas desde Francia.
Aquellas otras desde Sicilia
y las finales desde Clivio
han escapado
como palomas espantadas.
Créeme, esto no es un lamento.
Te escribo para conjurar mis sombras.

Third Letter

*I don't know why I write to you*


Since you don't deserve it
because of your lack of soul.
Your promised letters from France.
Those others from Sicily
and the last ones from Clivio
have escaped
like frightened doves.
Believe me, this is not a lament.
I write to you to exorcise my ghosts.

## Cuarta Carta

*El dolor de tu ausencia, quizás eterna, no apaga*
*el ímpetu de mi amor por ti*

Es cierto que a los hombres,
tú eres un buen ejemplo,
les gusta dejar amarse
por nosotras las mujeres.
Nosotras lo damos todo:
arriesgamos nombre y vida,
entregamos la posibilidad del tiempo
y hasta los sonidos de los sueños.
No mentí cuando te declaré mi amor.
Han pasado casi dos años
desde que me negaste tu presencia
y aún te hablo desde mi yo todo.

## Fourth Letter

*The pain of your absence, perhaps eternal, does
not extinguish the force of my love for you*


It is true that men,
you being a good example,
like to let us
women love them.
We give everything:
risking life and reputation,
offering the possibility of time
and even the sounds of dreams.
I did not lie when I declared my love to you.
Nearly two years have passed
since you denied me your presence
and still my whole being calls out to you.

## Quinta Carta

*Creo que no volveré a escribirte*

Por favor,
a caballo o *express mail*
envíame:
mis botas de nieve,
el pergamino de mi apellido,
todos los libros de S.B.,
y el daguerrotipo
de nuestra felicidad.

## Fifth Letter

*I think I shall not write to you again*

Please,
send me
by horse or express mail:
my snow boots,
the scroll of my family crest,
all the books of S.B.,
and the daguerreotype
of our happiness.

# Mi abuela era
## una curiosa mujer

*...el joven por el que yo sentía un total afecto (...)
era uno de esos seres fríos y calculadores, para los
cuales una gran pasión siempre revestía una
apariencia de locura: tuvo miedo de mi amor.*

*Flora Tristán*

A veces nosotras las mujeres
con un disfraz de indiferencia
nos hacemos reinas,
pero ustedes bien saben que
una declaración de amor
puede ser fatal:

-¡No me hagas daño!, me dijo "el joven" cuando
se encontró desnudo conmigo en el medio de
mis *Pérégrinations*:

—Amor mío, no me pidas cosas terribles.
Me voy al Perú en barco, no quiero sentir de
nuevo ni tu sudor, ni tu demencia de amor, ni
tus pensamientos.

## My Grandmother was
## a Peculiar Woman

*...the young man I loved completely (...) was one
of those cold and calculating beings, for whom a
great passion always bore the appearance of madness: he was afraid of my love.*

Flora Tristán

> Sometimes we women
> With  a disguise of indifference
> make ourselves queens,
> but you well know that
> a declaration of love
> can be fatal:

"Don't hurt me!" said the "young man" when he
found himself naked with me in the middle of
my *Peregrinations*:

"My love, don't ask me for terrible things.
I am going to Peru by boat, I do not want to see
again your sweat, your crazed love, or your
thoughts."

## Tres lindas cubanas

I
*...nosotras las habaneras, confesamos siempre mucho menos de lo que sentimos*

Condesa de Merlín, *Correspondencia íntima, 1842.*

## Diario al inconstante

Dejémonos de eufemismos
querido Victor Philarete
y vayamos al grano.
Tengo cincuenta años
y vivo de pedigüeña.
He vendido mi reloj y mi coche
y no tengo quien me peine.
Los impulsos de mi corazón
se quedaron en La Havane,
Baden, Metz y el castillo de Dissay.
Mi amor impetuoso por ti
se lo lleva la corriente
y "nuestra obra"
es esta pasión desesperada
de tu

*Mercedes*

# Three Lovely Cuban Ladies

I
*...we women of Havana always admit much less than we feel*

Countess of Merlin, *Private correspondance*, 1842.

## Diary to the Unfaithful One

Let's forget the euphemisms
dear Victor Philarete
and go straight to the point.
I am fifty years old
and live on handouts.
I have sold my watch and my carriage
and have no one to do my hair.
My heart's desires
were left in Havana,
Baden, Metz and the castle of Dissay.
The current has swept away
my impetuous love for you
and "our work"
is this desperate passion
of your

*Mercedes*

II

# Carta casi inédita
# a Antonio

*Te amo cuando no te veo, cuando no te escucho,*
*cuando solo llegan à mi tus cartas...*

*Tula*
*(rúbrica)*

Ni compromisos forzosos, ni confesiones
innecesarias quiero.
Mi libertad verdadera es no ser esclava
de nada ni de nadie.
Escribo cuando quiero, a pesar de mis infames
plumas,
y al final de mi vida defino el amor como
el querer escribirte una hora después de
habernos separado.

II

# Almost Unpublished Letter
# to Antonio

*I love you when I don't see you, when I don't*
*hear you, when I only receive your letters...*

*Tula*
*(seal)*

I want neither forced commitments, nor
unnecessary confessions.
My true freedom lies in not being a slave
to anyone or anything.
I write when I want to, in spite of my terrible
pens,
and at my life's end I define love as wanting to
write to you an hour after
we separate.

III

# 9 de la mañana de 1895

*Mi Carlos mío; hoy es miércoles... mañana es el día de las ilusiones ¡Mañana te veré! (...) Ayer noche puse en el correo cartas para ti. Desde el jueves no he dejado de escribir un sólo día. Alucinada y delirante en la cámara oscura de tus ojos* adivino mi porvenir y me suicido en cada palabra que escribo.

*Ivone-Juana*

III

# 9 in the Morning of 1895

*My own Carlos: today is Wednesday... tomorrow*
*is the day of my dreams. Tomorrow I'll see you!*
*(...) Last night I mailed letters to you. Since*
*Thursday I haven't let a single day go by without*
*writing to you.* Hallucinating and delirious *in the*
*camera obscura of your eyes* I foresee my future
and kill myself with every word I write.

*Ivone-Juana*

## Los pasos de la condesa

*No deseo ciertamente que me hagas una
infidelidad, no; pero aun concibo menos que te
eches una amiga espiritual, a quien le cuentes tus
argumentos de novelas.*

*(Fragmento de una carta de Emilia Pardo Bazán a
Benito Pérez Galdós)*

Entre 1889 y 1890
mi pluma te ha querido
como a nadie.
Me niego a aceptar
que los rumores
que andan por ahí
sean ciertos.
*verdad, mi alma,
¿que es imposible?*

# The Interludes of the Countess

*I certainly do not want you to be unfaithful to
me, no; but it is even harder for me to conceive
of your taking a woman as an intellectual friend
and telling her the plots of your novels.*

*(Passage from a letter of Emilia Pardo Bazán to
Benito Pérez Galdós)*

Between 1889 and 1890
my pen has loved you
as no other.
I refuse to believe
that the rumors
which are circulating
are true.
*It's impossible,
isn't it, my precious?*

## Wolfrathausen
## o el arte de la memoria

*(no necesites nada y haz lo que quieras)*

Quiero huir de tus manos que me queman y dejar que el trazo de tu pluma sea la poesía que me falta. Nunca había sentido la vida como ahora. Si todo lo que ves en el mundo es a través de mis ojos, disuélvete en mi, sé en mi, expulsa todo sueño donde yo no esté. Mírame con los ojos cerrados. Es ya hora de bendecir nuestros besos.

*(Lou Andreas-Salomé le escribe a Rilke, 189...)*

# Wolfrathausen
## or the Art of Memory

*(need nothing and do as you please)*

I want to flee from your hands which burn me
and let the stroke of your pen give me the
poetry I need. I never felt life the way I do now.
If everything you see in the world is through my
eyes, dissolve yourself in me, be in me, banish
every dream that does not include me. See me
with your eyes closed. It is time now to bless our
kisses.

*(Lou Andreas-Salomé writing to Rilke, 189...)*

## Carta de Rosa Luxemburgo
## a Leo Jögiches

*Dyodyu, querido mío (...) sí, tienes razón.
Hemos vivido vidas espirituales separadas por
mucho tiempo.* Mi soledad ha sido espantosa
estos dos últimos años. *Mi última visita a Zürich
me dejó sin la menor duda de que te has vuelto
totalmente ciego para mí, para mi ser interior,
que todo lo que soy para ti es una mujer más,
quizás diferente de las otras en el hecho de que
escribo* poemas.

Miles de besos

*R.*

## Letter from Rosa Luxemburg
## to Leo Jögiches

*Dyodyu, my love (...) yes, you are right. We have led separate spiritual lives for a long time.* My loneliness has been horrible these last two years. *My last visit to Zürich left me convinced that you have become completely blind to me, to my inner being, that I am just one more woman for you, perhaps different from the others by virtue of writing* poems.

Thousands of kisses

*R.*

## Each Love Affair in My Life
## Would Have Made a Novel

escribió Isadora Duncan.


Todas las mujeres somos músicos:
en cada hombre tocamos notas diferentes
y oímos melodías variadas.
¿Se pueden igualar acaso la música de Beethoven
y la de Cesar Franck?
¿Puedo acaso comparar el
"Prends moi, prends moi!"
de Gabriel D'Annunzio a las poesías que por tres
años Sergei Essenin me susurró al oído?

*And I suppose a woman who has known but
one man is like a person who has heard only
one composer.*

(1927)

## Each Love Affair in My Life Would Have Made a Novel

wrote Isadora Duncan.


All women are musicians:
we play different notes on each man
and we hear various melodies.
Can the music of Beethoven be the same
as that of Cesar Franck?
Can I possibly compare the
"Prends moi, prends moi!"
of Gabriel D'Annunzio to the poems that
Sergei Essenin whispered in my ear for three years?

*And I suppose a woman who has known but
one man is like a person who has heard only
one composer.*

(1927)

## Daguerrotipos
## y cartas olvidadas

En espera de las lluvias
empiezo a escribir los cuentos
que viviremos
tan pronto regreses.
*Nada puede compararse*
a esta *folie à deux.*

Tengo a Mozart y a Schubert
en la punta de mis dedos
mientras planto café o
cazo leones o hablo.

En espera de las lluvias
se manifiesta mi alegría
de lo porvenir.
Dibujo anagramas
,en el cristal de la ventana
que te verá llegar.
Ver "Out of Africa" contigo
fue creerme Isak Dinesen
e imaginarte Denys Finch-Hatton.

## Daguerreotypes
## and Forgotten Letters

Waiting for the rain
I begin to write the stories
we will live
as soon as you return.
Nothing can compare
to this *folie à deux.*

I have Mozart and Schubert
at my fingertips
while I plant coffee or
hunt lions or talk.

Waiting for the rain
my joy over the future
shows itself.
I draw anagrams
on the windowpane
that wil see you arrive.
To see "Out of Africa" with you
was to believe myself Isak Dinesen
and imagine you Denys Finch-Hatton.

## *Exilios: carta inédita de Nora*

Mi exilio está tejido en la tierra de KircheFlüntern
desde 1951: soy católica y que más da que me
llame Nora Barnacle si trabajo en el Finn's Hotel
de Leinster Street Dublin y Jim debía haberse
dedicado al canto y no a la escritura porque la
música hay qué diferencia esas páginas tan raras y
los escritores que gente qué gente en que Planeta
me muevo Jim si hubiera querido tener cartas
eróticas ese verano que me sentí tan sola y tú las
escribiste cuando lo necesitabas tú Trieste París o
Zürich todas la misma cosa tan provincianas que
no entienden el irlandés ni el español que hablo.

## *Exiles: Unpublished Letter from Nora*

Since 1951 my exile is woven into the land of
KircheFlüntern: I am a Catholic and what difference does it make that my name is Nora Barnacle
if I work in Finn's Hotel on Leinster Street
Dublin and Jim should have been a singer and
not a writer because there is music what a difference those strange pages and the writers what
people what people on the Planet on which I
move Jim if I had wanted to have erotic letters
that summer when I felt so alone and you wrote
them when you needed it Trieste, Paris or Zürich
all the same so provincial that they don't understand the Irish or the Spanish I speak.

## Carta de La Belle Otero
## a uno de sus biógrafos

Estimado admirador:

He perdido un poco la memoria, pero aún me acuerdo de que nací en Galicia un día de noviembre de 1868 y que me bautizaron bajo el nombre de Agustina. Mi familia era demasiado grande y de pocas ambiciones, mientras que yo era chiquita pero mis ambiciones grandes. Me enamoré, sí señor, de un mequetrefe que me hizo correr mundo..., perdone ud., pero hablar de mi misma es un acto audaz y no quiero aventurarme a distorsionar mi imagen. bueno, le contaba que ... debuté en un music hall de Manhattan en 1890 y conocí al amor de mi vida = Ernest Andrée Jurgens, ¡felices fueron aquellos tiempos! yo tan joven y bonita, él tan guapo, tan creador de leyendas..., después de hacerme famosa no he vuelto a saber lo que es la felicidad. El amor ha sido mi comercio. Me han acusado de no tener alma y de haber conocido a los partidos más ricos del mundo. Mi verdadera pasión ha sido el juego y mi enemiga, la pobreza (aunque bien pudiera mencionarle el nombre de algunas envidiosas que

## Letter from *La Belle Otero* to One of Her Biographers

Dear Admirer:

My memory is fading a bit, but I still remember I was born in Galicia on a November day in 1868 and was baptized with the name of Agustina. My family was too big and had few ambitions, whereas I was little but had big ambitions. I fell in love, yes sir, with a good-for-nothing who dragged me around the world..., pardon me, but it's audacious to talk about myself and I don't want to go so far as to distort my image. Well, I was telling you that... I made my debut in a music hall in Manhattan in 1890 and met the love of my life = Ernst Andrée Jurgens, what happy times those were! I so young and pretty, he so handsome, a real mythmaker.., once I became famous, I never again knew happiness. Love has been my business. I've been accused of being heartless and of having made the richest matches in the world. My true passion has been gambling, and my enemy, poverty (although I could well mention the names of some envious women who could have wished to see me turn into dust. I'm referring to hubieran querido verme hecha polvo, me refiero a la Cléo de Mérode y a la Liane de Pogny). He tenido buenos amigos. Nunca me olvidaré de lo que mi querida Colette escribió sobre mis pechos de limón. Si quiere algunas fotografías y recortes de periódicos, se los enviaré. Si por casualidad pasa por Niza, venga a verme porque me voy a morir el 10 de abril de 1965. Suya,

*Carolina*

Cléo de Mérode and Liane De Pogny). I have had good friends. I shall never forget what my dear Colette wrote about my lemon-shaped breasts. If you want any photographs or newspaper clippings, I'll send them to you. If by chance you are in Nice, stop by to see me because I am going to die on April 10, 1965. Yours,

*Carolina*

# En esta hora apacible y dulce

*¿Sabes que soy muy pesada de manos? Me gusta pegar; creo que acaricio y dejo una mancha. Las muchachas que viven conmigo dicen que mis palomas (las manos) son en verdad gavilanes...*

*(Carta de Gabriela Mistral a Manuel Magallanes)*

Manuel, esta es mi carta XXVI
y sigo disfrutando este hablarte.
Me hubiera gustado ver la tarde contigo
y ser dichosa y tener paz y quererte.

## In this Sweet and Peaceful Moment

*Do you know, I'm very heavy-handed? I like to hit; I think I'm caressing and I leave a mark. The girls who live with me say that my doves (my hands) are really hawks...*

*(Letter from Gabriela Mistral to Manuel Magallanes)*

Manuel, this is my XXVI letter
and I continue to relish talking to you.
I would have liked to see the sunset with you
and be happy and at peace loving you.

## Autorretrato

Tus ojos, verdes dentro de mi carne. Todo tú en el espacio lleno de sonidos, en la sombra y en la luz.

*(Carta de Frida Kahlo a Diego Rivera)*

Duermo en tus axilas
y soy número perdido
entre combinaciones.
Abrazo el universo
cada vez que te acaricio.
Quiero ser todas las mujeres que amas.
Quiero engendrarte de nuevo.
*Perderte es impensable. Lo eres todo.*

# Self-Portrait

*Your eyes, green within my flesh. All of you in
the sound-filled space, in the shadows and in the
light.*

*(Letter from Frida Kahlo to Diego Rivera)*

I sleep in your armpits
and I am a number lost
among many.
I embrace the universe
every time I caress you.
I want to be all the women you love.
I want to give birth to you again.
*To lose you is unthinkable. You are everything.*

## *Stolen Kisses are the Sweetest,*
*Louveciennes, 1932*

*Henry:*

*Je pense à toi tous le temps.*

*Anaïs*

Lo único que quiero saber es
si detrás del espejo
me esperan tus ojos.
Kiss me quick, my dear,
que la vida es breve.

Te amo ha tomado por asalto
todos mis *Diarios.*
Veámonos dónde y cómo sea.
Quiero que tus manos
escriban en los pliegues
de mis páginas,
todas tus aventuras,
y que cada trazo de tu pluma
sirva para hacer
menos virgen mi cuaderno.

## Stolen Kisses are the Sweetest,
### Louveciennes, 1932

*Henry:*

*Je pense à toi tous le temps.*

*Anaïs*

The only thing I want to know is
if behind the mirror
your eyes wait for me.
Kiss me quick, my dear,
for life is short.

I love you has taken over
all my *Diaries.*
Let us meet whenever and however we can.
I want your hands
to write all your adventures
in the folds
of my pages,
so that each stroke of your pen
will make
my notebook less virginal.

# A Well-Tempered Journey

I

## If I could kiss your sweet mouth and eat green poached eggs with pepper

*Querido:*

*Tu carta me parece tan absurda que por más que la leo no puedo creer que después de habernos amado tanto me digas que sólo puedes darme tu amistad. ¿No quieres compromisos? Yo tampoco. ¿Tienes miedos? Yo también. Lee mi carta con cuidado. No puedo pedirte que seas lo que no eres, ni que me ames si no lo sientes, pero déjame saber al menos lo que te hizo cambiar respecto a mi. Trata de entender que yo no he cambiado y aún pienso en ti y en nuestros paseos a las montañas, y en nuestras lecturas antes de dormir, en nuestro deambular por las calles, en nuestros viajes en tren, y en ese nuestro siempre celebrar la vida. Sólo te pido que pienses en la posibilidad de reanudar nuestros diálogos. No temas. Tenemos todas las de ganar. Con todo mi amor,*

*Yo.*

# A Well-Tempered Journey

I

## If I could kiss your sweet mouth and eat green poached eggs with pepper

*Dearest:*

*I find your letter so absurd that as much as I read it I still can't believe after loving each other so much you now tell me you can only give me friendship. You don't want obligations? I don't either. You are fearful? I am too. Read my letter carefully. I can't ask you to be what you are not, or to love me if you don't feel it, but at least let me know what made you change your attitude toward me. Try to understand that I have not changed and I still think of you and our walks in the mountains, and reading together before bed, and strolling in the streets, and our train trips, and our constant celebration of life. I only ask that you think of renewing our dialogues. Don't be afraid. We have everything to gain. With all my love,*

*Me.*

II

*(Si yo fuera como tú,*
*si fueras como yo)*

Sin remitente

La música del mediodía me dejó sin virtud: *"el*
*agua horada la roca a fuerza de caer en ella"* y
pensé que quizás podíamos cambiar los papeles.
Máscaras de Venecia, viento que sopla dentro de
mí, toda mirada a tu cuerpo desnudo prohibida,
porque soy el monje de la montaña y yo un canal
desbordado y yo sufro y yo no sé lo que tengo y
yo siento tus latidos y yo de pronto tocando un
preludio y fuga de Bach en lo que nunca podrás
ni quieres darme y yo desesperado porque tengo
miedo y yo hambrienta de tu aliento y yo casi
lloro y me niego a tus manos y yo esperando y yo
dejo de ser, el terror me invade, y yo soy tú ahora
y te quiero, no tengas miedo mi amor, mi amor
que no sé de violencias, no te inquietes, yo soy la
que te adora ángel, espiga, la que soy fuerte, y mi
mano bajo estas sábanas de hilo te lleva en este
viaje bien templado hasta las aguas de Dios: esta
es la puerta de la bendición.

II

## (If I were Like You,
## If You Were Like Me)

No return address

The noon music left me powerless: *"the falling water wears away rock"* and I thought perhaps we could change roles. Venetian Masks, wind blowing within me, any glance at your naked body is prohibited, because I am the monk of the mountain and I an overflowing canal and I suffer and I don't know what I have and I feel your heartbeat and suddenly I am playing a Bach prelude and fugue in what you can never give or wish to give me and I desperate because of fear and I hungry for your breath and I almost cry and refuse your hands and I wait and I cease to be, the terror invades me, and now I am you and I love you, do not be afraid my love, my love I know nothing of violence, do not be troubled, I am the one who adores you angel, wheat stalk, the one who is strong, and my hand beneath these linen sheets takes you on this finely tuned trip to God's waters: this is the doorway to blessedness.

## *Texturas enviadas a T. vía e-mail*

La presente es sólo para decirte que
iré a San Francisco mañana.
Espérame a la 11 a.m. y no te olvides
de Cornelius.
Hace frío en Oakland
y dibujo en tu cuerpo.

## Textures Sent to T. by e-mail

This is only to tell you
I am going to San Francisco tomorrow.
Wait for me at 11 a.m. and don't forget
about Cornelius.
It is cold in Oakland
and I am sketching on your body.

# About the Author

CARLOTA CAULFIELD is a Cuban Poet. She is the author of nine books of poetry, including *34th Street and other poems*, with a preface by Jack Foley, *Angel Dust/Polvo de Angel/Polvere D'Angelo* and *Book of the XXXIX steps. A poetry game of discovery and imagination.* Hyperbook for the Macintosh. Her work has appeared in *Visions, Michigan Quarterly Review, Beacons, The Texas Review, Haight Ashbury Literary Journal, Puente Libre, Brújula/Compass, Nómada, Inti, Poetry San Francisco, and Walrus.* She was awarded the International poetry prize, "Ultimo Novecento," in Italy (1988), the "Plural Prize" Honorable Mention in Mexico City (1993), the International Poetry Prize "Federico García Lorca," Honorable Mention (Spain-USA-1994), the International Poetry Prize "Riccardo Marchi-Torre di Calafuria," in Italy (1995), and the "1997 Latino Literature Prize" Honorable Mention of the Latin American Writers Institute of New York.

Visit her web page at
http://www.intelinet.org/Caulfield

Her works as editor include *Literary and Cultural Journeys: Selected Letters to Arturo Torres-Rioseco* and *Web of Memories. Interviews with Five Cuban Poets.* Caulfield is the editor of *CORNER*, http://www.cornermag.org, a journal dedicated to the avant-garde. She teaches at Mills College.

# About the Translator

ANGELA McEWAN's recent literary translations include *Irene*, a novel by Jorge Eliecer Pardo (Research UP, 2000) and the story "La llamada/The Call" by Ciro Alegría in *Amazonian Literary Review*, Issue 2, 1999. In *Luz en arte y literatura*, a bilingual literary review, No. 12, 1999: "Botánica poética/Poetic Herbarium" by Carlota Caulfield. She translated a poetry collection by Verónica Miranda, *Más allá de una vez/More Than Once* in Carpetas de Luz, 1999, and poems from "Punto Umbrío" in *Hubo un tiempo/There Was A Time*, an anthology of Ana Rossetti's poems, edited by Yolanda Rosas and Teresa Rozo-Moorhouse (Ediciones Latidos, 1997). She also translated Caulfield's *Libro de los XXXIX escalones* into English, published by Luz Bilingual in 1997.

# Colophon

Type composition for this book was accomplished on a Power Macintosh G3 computer in Goudy Old Style type.

In 1915, Frederic W. Goudy designed Goudy Old Style, his twenty-fifth typeface, and his first for American Type Founders. Flexible enough for both text and display, it is one of the most popular typefaces ever produced. Its recognizable features include the diamond-shaped dots on i, j, and on punctuation marks; the upturned ear of the g; and the base of E and L.

Several years later, in response to the overwhelming popularity of Cooper Black, Lanston Monotype commissioned Frederic W. Goudy to design heavy versions of Goudy Old Style. Goudy Heavyface and Goudy Heavyface Italic were released in 1925. The huge success of Goudy's typefaces led to the addition of several weights to many of his typefaces; designers working for American Type Founders produced additions to the family. In 1927, Morris Fuller Benton drew Goudy Extra Bold.

Printed in the United States
3456

9 780971 139121